HARD
OF HISTORY
Ancient
Greece

TRACEY TURNER
ILLUSTRATED BY JAMIE LENMAN

A & C BLACK
AN IMPRINT OF BLOOMSBURY
LONDON   NEW DELHI   NEW YORK   SYDNEY

First published 2014 by

A & C Black, an imprint of Bloomsbury Publishing Plc

50 Bedford Square, London WC1B 3DP

www.bloomsbury.com

Copyright © 2014 A & C Black

Text copyright © 2014 Tracey Turner

Illustrations copyright © 2014 Jamie Lenman
Additional images © Shutterstock

ISBN 978-1-4729-0562-8

A CIP catalogue for this book is available from the British Library.

This book is produced using paper that is made from wood grown in managed, sustainable forests. It is natural, renewable and recyclable. The logging and manufacturing processes conform to the environmental regulations of the country of origin.

Printed in China by Leo Paper Products, Heshan, Guangdong

1 3 5 7 9 10 8 6 4 2

CONTENTS

20KM
TO
ATHENS

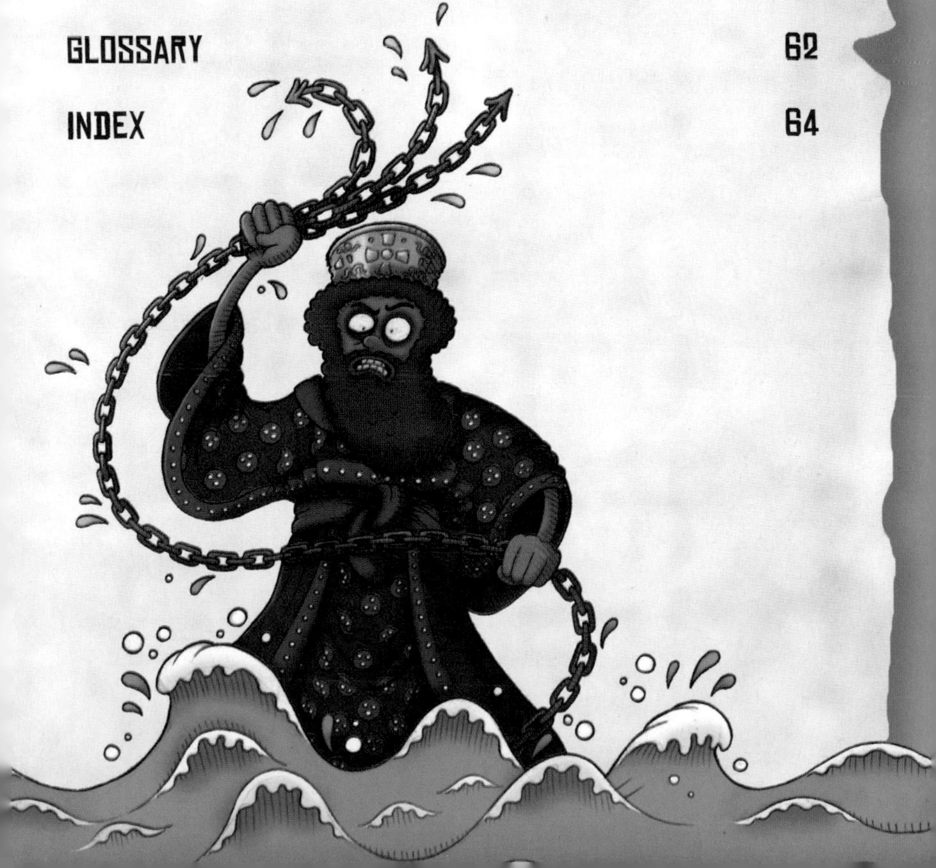

INTRODUCTION

This book contains some of the hardest nuts of ancient Greece, from brave Spartan warriors to pondering Athenian philosophers. Some of them were courageous, some were clever, some were fearsome fighters, and some were absolutely awful. But all of them were as hard as nails.

FIND OUT ABOUT . . .

• An ancient family curse

• Cruel, power-crazed tyrants

• A nine-headed water snake

• Burning death rays that set fire to ships

If you've ever wanted to discover the meaning of life, join the terrifyingly tough Spartan army, or invade Sicily, read on. Follow the hard nuts on the first marathon ever, to the bloody battlefields of the Peloponnese, and aboard a Persian warship in the Mediterranean Sea.

As well as discovering stories of courage and cunning, you might be in for a few surprises. Did you know, for example, that Alexander the Great named a city after his horse? Or that Persian King Xerxes was so cross with the sea that he had it whipped with chains?

You're about to meet some of the toughest people of ancient Greece. . .

CLEISTHENES

Cleisthenes became famous for his politics, but first he had to battle a power-crazed tyrant, a ruthless rival, and an ancient family curse . . .

HARD NUT RATING: 7.5

CLEISTHENES' CURSE

Cleisthenes was born in Athens around 570 BC into a posh family, which, unfortunately, had a curse upon it. Cleisthenes' great-grandfather had killed political rivals who had taken refuge in a temple – he'd broken his promise to keep them safe. As a result Cleisthenes' family was cursed and thrown out of Athens. They were eventually allowed back, but got chucked out again every so often because of the curse.

HIPPIAS THE TYRANT

Hippias was Athens' tyrant. In those days, 'tyrant' meant an absolute ruler, like a king, and didn't necessarily mean a cruel megalomaniac . . . but in Hippias' case, it did. Cleisthenes managed to get rid of horrible Hippias, with help from his extended family. But then Cleisthenes was sent into exile by his political rival Isagoras and his Spartan friends. The excuse for getting rid of Cleisthenes was the family curse, which had come back to haunt him again.

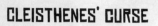

HARDOMETER

CUNNING: 9
COURAGE: 7
SURVIVAL SKILLS: 8
RUTHLESSNESS: 6

ISAGORAS GETS NASTY

Isagoras made himself very unpopular, partly by announcing that various families were cursed and sending them into exile – after all, it had worked so well with Cleisthenes – and partly by trying to get rid of a long-established Athenian council. The people of Athens decided they wanted Isagoras out, and rioted. They trapped Isagoras and his supporters on the Acropolis, and ruthlessly killed the lot – though Isagoras managed to escape. Cleisthenes was called back to Athens and elected 'archon', the top job in Athenian politics.

CLEISTHENES TAKES CHARGE

Cleisthenes decided to make things fairer and change the way Athens was run: he divided people up into groups according to where they lived instead of family ties, and made other changes like reorganising the law-courts. His changes encouraged more people to become involved in politics than ever before, and he introduced the idea of equal rights for all. After he died, Cleisthenes became known as the father of Athenian democracy.

EXILE

GREEK CITY-STATES

The people who lived in ancient Greece didn't call themselves ancient Greeks – not even the really old people. They didn't think of themselves as living in Greece, but rather in Athens, or Sparta, or one of the other Greek city-states (the Greek name for a city-state is polis, which is how we get our word 'politics').

The Greeks all spoke the same language, and had the same religion and myths, so they had quite a lot in common. Sometimes they joined together to fight a common enemy, and sometimes they fought one another. The two most powerful city-states during Greece's classical period were Athens and Sparta.

ATHENS

Athens had an unusual (for ancient times) system of government: citizens were ruled by elected leaders and had a say in how they were governed. In fact, it was expected that all Athenian citizens should take an active role in government and law. Not everyone was a citizen, though – women, foreigners and slaves (and there were a lot of these) were not classed as citizens.

SPARTA

Sparta was ruled by two kings and a council of elders, and had the most powerful army in all of Greece. Male Spartan citizens were trained to be especially tough fighters. Like Athens, Sparta relied on slaves – Spartan slaves were called helots, and once a year it was acceptable for Spartans to kill them! No wonder they sometimes rebelled. Sparta and Athens joined together to fight against the Persian invaders, along with several other Greek city-states, but went to war with one another in the Peloponnesian War.

OTHER CITY-STATES

There were hundreds of other city-states throughout Greece. Corinth was a wealthy city-state, which was on the same side as Sparta in the Peloponnesian War, but later fought against Sparta. Syracuse on the island of Sicily was a Corinthian colony. The city-state of Thebes joined forces with the Persians when they invaded Greece in 480 BC, but fought with Sparta against Athens in the Peloponnesian War. Eventually Thebes defeated Sparta and became the most powerful city-state in ancient Greece in the 300s BC.

ALEXANDER THE GREAT

HARD NUT RATING: 8.3

Alexander the Great was a rampaging conqueror who founded dozens of cities, defeated an empire and created an enormous new one of his own.

KING ALEXANDER

Alexander's father, King Philip II of Macedonia, was assassinated in 336 BC, and Alexander, who was 20 years old, became King. Philip had made Macedonia powerful: it controlled most of Greece and had a huge, well-trained army. After Philip's death Alexander began by killing his father's murderers and any rivals to the throne, and ruthlessly crushing a Greek uprising in Thebes. But Alexander didn't stop there and looked outside his own lands: he had plans for expansion.

BATTLING THE PERSIANS

Darius III ruled the mighty Persian Empire, which stretched from Asia Minor (modern-day Turkey) around the Mediterranean and into Egypt. Alexander set about grabbing the empire for himself at the Battle of Issus. Alexander's army battered the Persians even though the Persian army was more than twice the size of theirs. Darius ran away, and met Alexander again at the Battle of Gaugamela. This time, Alexander defeated the Persians completely, and was proclaimed Great King of Asia.

HARDOMETER

CUNNING: 8
COURAGE: 8
SURVIVAL SKILLS: 8
RUTHLESSNESS: 9

CONQUERING EVERYONE ELSE

Alexander marched into Babylon, where he did a lot of celebrating, then on to Susa, the capital city of Persia (modern-day Iran), gathering treasure as he went. He carried on conquering through Central Asia and into what's now Pakistan and India. In India, he defeated King Poros, whose army rode into battle on elephants. But by this time, Alexander's army felt that they'd done enough conquering and wanted to go home, so Alexander turned back.

NO MORE CONQUERING

By the end of Alexander's conquering days his huge empire stretched from the Mediterranean to the Himalayas. He celebrated his victories with lots of massive parties. However, after one party he became ill and died, at the age of just 32. In the 12 years he'd been king he'd founded more than 70 cities. Many of them were called Alexandria, but he named one Bucephalia, after his trusty warhorse Bucephalus.

BUCEPHALIA
ALEXANDRIA
ALEXANDRIA
ALEXANDRIA
ALEXANDRIA
ALEXANDRIA
ALEXANDRIA
ALEXANDRIA
ALEXANDRIA
ALEXANDRIA
ALEXANDRIA
ALEXANDRIA
ALEXANDRIA
ALEXANDRIA
ALEXANDRIA
ALEXANDRIA
ALEXANDRIA
ALEXANDRIA
ALEXANDRIA
ALEXANDRIA
ALEXANDRIA
ALEXANDRIA
ALEXANDRIA
ALEXANDRIA

LEONIDAS

Leonidas became legendary for his astonishing courage while defending Greece from the Persians against all odds.

PRINCE LEONIDAS

Leonidas was born in the city state of Sparta, the son of the Spartan king, and like all well-born Spartan boys, he went to a hard-nut boarding school from the age of seven, where he learned how to be a tremendously tough Spartan warrior. Leonidas then became king around 490 BC.

THOSE PESKY PERSIANS

The Persians wanted to make Greece part of their empire, and had already tried to invade. In 480 BC, Persian leader King Xerxes I was plotting another invasion and he had a huge army and navy at the ready – this time he really meant business. But Leonidas planned to stop the Persians at Thermopylae, a pass between the mountains and the sea, and so took charge of an army of allied Greeks.

OUTNUMBERED

Leonidas and the Greeks were massively outnumbered, probably by about ten to one, and Leonidas could see that his only chance of stopping the Persians was to defend the narrowest part of the pass. The Persians sent him a message saying something along the lines of, 'You and your pathetic little army don't stand a chance – surrender and lay down your weapons.' Leonidas replied by saying something like, 'Come and get them – if you think you're hard enough.'

SECRET PASS

Leonidas and his men were so tough that they held back the huge Persian army. Unfortunately, a sneaky traitor told the Persians about a secret pass through the mountains. Once Leonidas discovered he'd been betrayed he realised that as soon as the Persians got through the secret pass, the Greek army would be massacred. He sent most of the men to safety, then fought on with about 1,500 of his hardest soldiers, all of whom knew they faced certain death.

DEFEAT . . . AND VICTORY

Leonidas and his soldiers all died fighting the Persians. But their bravery and self-sacrifice made them famous. Lots of Persians died in the battle too, and the army never quite recovered from it. Even though the Persians had won, the following year they were sent packing from Greece for good.

HARDOMETER

CUNNING: 7
COURAGE: 10
SURVIVAL SKILLS: 6
RUTHLESSNESS: 7

PERSIANS AND THE PELOPONNESE

THE PERSIAN WARS

The Persian Wars began in 499 BC and went on until 449 BC. Persia had a massive empire that stretched from the Mediterranean Sea to the Indus River valley, including Greek cities in Asia Minor (now Turkey) and some Greek islands. Greece was next.

Even though Greece was tiny compared to the Persian Empire, Sparta had an army of terrifyingly tough warriors, and Athens had a quick and crafty navy that made them unbeatable at sea. Other city-states joined them in the fight against the Persians. There were three major battles during the Persian Wars – Marathon, Thermopylae and Salamis (see pages 46, 14, 28), and in each one the Persians were thwarted (even if they weren't completely defeated). They never managed to grab Greece.

THE PELOPONNESIAN WAR

Twenty years after the end of the Persian Wars, the Greeks were at it again, this time fighting amongst themselves. The Peloponnesian War is named after the Peloponnese, the big peninsula that included Sparta and other ancient city-states (the Peloponnesian League), who fought the Athenian Empire from 431 BC to 404 BC.

There was an uneasy peace in the middle of the war, but it didn't last long. In the end Sparta had help from the Persians (them again!), and finally Athens surrendered. Athens never rose to be a great power again, and civil war amongst the Greek city-states became common. The ancient Greek 'golden age' was over.

LYSANDER

Lysander was the hard-nut commander of the Spartan fleet that defeated Athens and finally ended the Peloponnesian War.

HARD NUT
RATING: 8.5

HUMBLE BEGINNINGS

Lysander's family were Heracleidae, a group of Spartans who claimed their ancestor was the ancient Greek mythical hero Heracles (see page 36). The family must have fallen on hard times, because Lysander needed to be sponsored by a rich Spartan in order to go to the tough military boarding school, the agoge, where he learned how to be a hard-as-nails Spartan warrior.

ADMIRAL OF THE FLEET

Lysander must have done really well, because in 407 BC (we don't know how old he was at the time) he got the top job of navarch, or admiral, of the Spartan fleet. The Spartans were keen on war and at the time the Peloponnesian War was raging between Sparta and Athens. Lysander set about creating a Spartan fleet capable of fighting the mighty Athenian fleet at Ephesus. At the Battle of Notium, he defeated the Athenian (and later Spartan) general Alcibiades (see page 32).

HARDOMETER

CUNNING: 9
COURAGE: 8
SURVIVAL SKILLS: 9
RUTHLESSNESS: 8

LYSANDER FIGHTS AGAIN

Lysander didn't stay in his job for long. After he'd left, the Athenians won a big battle against the Spartan navy, and the Spartans decided they needed Lysander's brilliant leadership again. Spartan law didn't allow the same navarch to hold the job twice, and it was very strict about its rules, so Lysander became deputy admiral. But everyone knew that he was really in charge.

SPARTA WINS

Lysander sailed the Spartan fleet to the Hellespont, a narrow, 60-kilometre-long stretch of sea that links the Mediterranean with the Sea of Marmaris. At the Battle of Aegospotami, Lysander and the Spartans defeated the Athenians, and for good measure captured Byzantium (which is now the city of Istanbul), Chalcedon and the island of Lesbos.

The Spartan King Pausinas besieged Athens, and Lysander's fleet blockaded its port. Athens had no choice: they surrendered, and Sparta won the Peloponnesian War.

NAVARCH

DEPUTY ADMIRAL

...TES

...asn't a fighter, but a
...inker. He stuck to his principles
even though it meant his own
execution.

STONEMASON AND SOLDIER

Socrates was born around 470 BC. His family wasn't
particularly rich or posh – his mother was a midwife, and
his father was a stonemason and sculptor, and for a while
that's what Socrates did too. He also served as a soldier in
the Athenian army, and according to another philosopher,
Plato, he saved the life of Alcibiades (see page 32) during a
battle with Corinth, another Greek city-state.

THINKING

Socrates gave up being a mason when he decided that the
most important thing of all was thinking, working out what
life meant, and how to live well – philosophy. He wandered
around Athens talking to people, asking questions and
thinking deep thoughts. Athens was a good place to be a
philosopher, because thinking and studying was generally
encouraged.

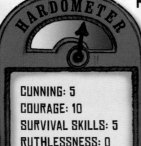

HARDOMETER

CUNNING: 5
COURAGE: 10
SURVIVAL SKILLS: 5
RUTHLESSNESS: 0

FRIENDS AND ENEMIES

Socrates held strong opinions
and he wasn't shy about letting
everyone know about them. He
thought that political leaders
should be especially wise and
clever, and if he didn't think
they were, he said so – loudly.
This made him very unpopular
with some of the people in

charge. He didn't believe in the gods and he also disagreed strongly with anyone who thought money and physical beauty were the most important things. Although he had plenty of friends, he made a lot of influential enemies too.

HORRIBLE HEMLOCK

Socrates' enemies charged him with being disrespectful to the gods and corrupting young people. Socrates could probably have got off the charges if he hadn't stuck to his guns quite so strongly, but he did, and he was sentenced to death as a result. His friends were horrified. They offered to bribe the guards and help him escape from Athens – and they would almost certainly have succeeded. But Socrates insisted that he should abide by his principles, and by the laws of Athens, and took his punishment. He was given the poison hemlock to drink, and died.

ANCIENT GREEK PHILOSOPHERS

Do you seek truth, wisdom, and the secrets of the universe? Do you question the nature of reality? Want to know everything about . . . well, everything? If so, you should definitely become a philosopher.

The ancient Greeks weren't the first to ask these sorts of questions, but they were the first to put a name to trying to answer them: philosophy, which means 'love of wisdom'. As well as asking questions about the meaning of life, ancient Greek philosophy included mathematics and science.

The three most famous Greek philosophers are Socrates (see page 20), Plato and Aristotle. The Epicureans, the Stoics and the Skeptics were three philosophical schools that came after Socrates, Plato and Aristotle. There were lots of other kinds too. Decide which of these ideas about life you most agree with, and find out which kind of philosopher you are.

PLATO

SOCRATES

1 You seek inner peace through moderation in everything – don't eat too much or work too much. But don't eat too little or laze around either. Accept what the world gives you rather than striving after things.

2 What can we ever really know about the world, or even about ourselves? And if we don't know much about that, how can we know what's right or wrong? It's better to just relax and leave everything in the hands of the gods.

3 To be happy, it's best not to want anything, because when we can't get what we want it makes us sad. The gods don't really affect people's lives, and when our bodies die so do our souls, so there's no reason to fear either the gods or death.

If you agree with 1... You're a Stoic. The Stoics were founded by the philosopher Zeno in the 200s BC. Today, you can be described as 'stoical' if you put up with hardship without complaining.

ARISTOTLE

If you agree with 2... You're a Skeptic. Pyrrhon started this school of philosophy in the 300s BC. He started from the idea that we can't rely on our senses to tell us the truth about things. Now, a 'sceptic' is someone who doubts accepted opinions.

If you agree with 3... You're an Epicurean. Epicurus founded his school in Athens in 307 BC. The word 'epicure' is used today to mean someone who likes the poshest food and drink, although Epicurus wasn't after pleasure, but freedom from pain and anxiety.

HYPATIA

Hypatia was a rare thing in the ancient world – a woman in charge. She was also the leading mathematician and astronomer of her time.

HARD NUT
RATING: 6.3

GREECE, EGYPT AND ROME

Hypatia was Greek, but born in Alexandria in Egypt around AD 355 to 370. By that time Alexandria was part of the Roman Empire, so Hypatia was a sort of Greek-Egyptian-Roman. Her father was a mathematician, and Hypatia became one too, as well as an astronomer and a philosopher.

HEAD TEACHER

By around AD 400 Hypatia was head of the Platonist school in Alexandria, a city known for its scholars. Today we're used to female teachers and lecturers, but in those days it was extremely unusual. Hypatia must have been a brilliant teacher as well as a tough nut to become head of one of the best colleges in the world.

TURBULENT TIMES

HARDOMETER

CUNNING: 5
COURAGE: 9
SURVIVAL SKILLS: 6
RUTHLESSNESS: 5

The governor of Alexandria, Orestes, was constantly arguing with the bishop of Alexandria, Cyril. Cyril was a Christian bishop, and in those days Christians were cross about having been persecuted for a long time – and some of them (Cyril included) were keen to get their own back. However, the rows between Cyril and Orestes were really about who was in control of the city. A group of Cyril-supporting angry monks stormed into the city and one of them hit Orestes on the head with a rock. As a result, the monk was tortured to death – and the fight became even worse.

MURDER MOST FOUL

A clever, female hard nut like Hypatia probably represented everything that was wrong with the world to a lot of the early Christians: she was a non-Christian thinker, a scientist and – perhaps most shocking of all – a woman! She was also a friend of Orestes. So one day in AD 415 a mob of murderous Christians kidnapped Hypatia and killed her. Her death was extremely gruesome.

ANCIENT GREEK WOMEN

Ancient Greece was an unusual period of history, because there were very few women about. Not really. But you might have thought so from the number of women in this book – just the one, and she lived a bit later than most of the other ancient Greeks.

UNEQUAL OPPORTUNITIES

There definitely were just as many women in ancient Greece as you'd expect there to be. But they weren't allowed to do the same kinds of things as the men – such as giving rousing political speeches, writing plays, becoming famous philosophers, fighting battles, or getting rich. They weren't even allowed to become citizens or vote. Athenian women – at least, the ones in wealthier homes – even had separate living quarters from the men. They were expected to look after the home and have children.

SPARTAN GIRL POWER

Things were a bit different in Sparta, where people thought about war first and everything else second. Men had to be tough warriors, and women had to produce boys who'd grow up to be tough warriors. That meant women had to be fit and healthy, so they did lots of sports and were just as fit as the men. They were also educated, unlike the girls in Athens. While the men were away (fighting, obviously), the women of Sparta had more of a say in running the city-state. Although they still weren't allowed to be citizens, Spartan women could own land, and some of them even became rich.

CHARIOT RACING

For example, Cynisca was a Spartan princess who entered her own chariot team in the Olympic games – and won, twice (in 396 and 392 BC). However, she didn't drive it (that kind of stuff was still left to the men), even though she was said to be a brilliant horse rider. She probably wouldn't have even watched her chariot win because there were no women allowed at the Olympics (partly because the men all competed absolutely stark naked). Cynisca was the first woman to win a chariot race, but other women followed in later years.

THEMISTOCLES

Themistocles was an Athenian leader who created and commanded a great navy, and saved Greece from the clutches of the invading Persians.

HARD NUT RATING: 8.5

INVADING PERSIANS

In 493 BC, when Themistocles was around 31 years old, he was elected chief archon in Athens, which was the top political job. Three years later, he was at the Battle of Marathon (see page 46) fighting the huge and terrifying Persian army. The Greeks won and everyone breathed a huge sigh of relief (especially in Athens). Many people thought that that was the end of the war. But Themistocles was suspicious.

THEMISTOCLES' NAVY

Themistocles thought that Athens should make itself invincible at sea, as a defence against the Persians. It wasn't easy, but he managed to persuade the people of Athens to use the money from a newly discovered silver mine to pay for 200 new warships for its navy.

HARDOMETER

CUNNING: 9
COURAGE: 9
SURVIVAL SKILLS: 7
RUTHLESSNESS: 9

XERXES ATTACKS

Themistocles was right to worry about Persia. The Persian King Xerxes I (see page 48) was planning a second invasion of Greece. At Themistocles' suggestion, the people of Athens were evacuated to the nearby island of Salamis, which could then be protected by the

Greek fleet, including the new warships as well as ships from other Greek city-states.

THE BATTLE OF SALAMIS

The allied Greek navy met the much larger Persian fleet at Salamis in 480 BC. But despite the greater number of Persian ships, the Greeks defeated the Persians. The victory was thanks to Themistocles' tactics and the new Athenian warships. It was the beginning of the end of Persia's invasion plans.

THEMISTOCLES GETS THE BOOT

Even though he'd saved Greece from the Persians, Themistocles ended up exiled, and accused of conspiring with the Persians. Ironically, he had to run away to live in Persian territory, where he became a Persian governor. He died in 462 BC. One story says that he poisoned himself in order to avoid having to help the Persians against Athens.

ARCHIMEDES

Archimedes is the most famous ancient Greek inventor and mathematician. He invented war machines, and was so hard that he refused to be bothered by rampaging Roman soldiers.

HARD NUT
RATING: 6.3

GREEKS IN SICILY

Archimedes was born between 290 and 280 BC in Syracuse, a city on the island of Sicily, and lived there for most of his life. Now Sicily is part of Italy, but then it was a Greek city-state. Since it was dangerously close to the capital city of the Roman Empire, the ancient Romans had their eye on it.

NAKED DISCOVERIES

After going to school in Alexandria in Egypt, Archimedes spent the rest of his life exercising his mighty brain on matters such as geometry, maths, and inventing. He's supposed to have invented the Archimedean Screw, and came up with the principle of the lever. According to legend, he was having a bath when he made

EUREKA!

his famous discoveries about how things float, and how much fluid an object displaces, and the weight of the displaced fluid. He's supposed to have shouted 'Eureka!' and gone running down the street without any clothes on!

ARCHIMEDES' DEADLY WEAPONS

The Romans attacked Sicily in 214 BC. Archimedes did his bit to defend Sicily by inventing some cunning weapons of war. These included a catapult, and a system of mirrors for focusing the sun's rays and setting fire to invading boats – although the fiery mirrors might be just a story.

ROMAN CONQUERORS

Despite Archimedes' weapons, the Romans won. The story goes that one of the conquering Roman soldiers came across Archimedes on the beach, where he was drawing diagrams in the sand and quite possibly just about to come up with another ground-breaking discovery. Archimedes told the soldier not to disturb his diagram, and the soldier responded by killing him with his sword.

SPHERES AND CYLINDERS

Archimedes' great brain would never come up with another invention or discovery. He was so proud of one discovery – about spheres, cylinders and their volumes and surface areas – that he asked for a diagram of it to be carved on his tomb.

HARDOMETER

CUNNING: 8
COURAGE: 8
SURVIVAL SKILLS: 5
RUTHLESSNESS: 4

ALCIBIADES

Alcibiades was a hard nut who had everything: looks, brains, money – and a tendency to switch sides when things weren't going well!

HARD NUT
RATING: 7.8

FAMOUS FRIENDS AND FAMILY

Alcibiades was born around 450 BC in Athens. After his father died, the famous politician Pericles (see page 40), brought him up. He grew up to be strong, clever, and amazingly good-looking. He became a friend of the philosopher Socrates (see page 20), with whom he fought bravely in battles between Athens and neighbouring city-states.

ATHENIAN ALCIBIADES

Athens and Sparta were at war during the time Alcibiades became a politician and general. Alcibiades tried and failed to organise an anti-Spartan alliance with other city-states, but he succeeded in persuading the Athenians to send troops to attack Syracuse in Sicily – a colony of Corinth, Sparta's ally.

HARDOMETER

CUNNING: 9
COURAGE: 5
SURVIVAL SKILLS: 8
RUTHLESSNESS: 9

DISASTERS

While he was sailing to Sicily, Alcibiades was accused of attacking statues of the gods in Athens, and saying rude things about religion. Worse still, the expedition to Sicily turned out to be a total disaster for the Athenians. They were well and truly battered, and thousands of soldiers and hundreds of ships were lost. Alcibiades promised to sail back to Athens, but instead sneaked off to help his Spartan enemies, who welcomed him with open arms. Unfortunately, so did the Spartan king's wife, and Alcibiades was exiled from Sparta in 412 BC.

PERSIA AND ATHENS AGAIN

Alcibiades ran away to Asia Minor (now Turkey), which was ruled by Athens' old enemy, Persia. He contacted the Athenians, promising them money and Persian ships if they were friendly towards him. Even though he'd betrayed them, the Athenians did ask him to come back. He led victories against the Spartans, but in 407 BC the Athenians chucked him out after a defeat in a sea battle.

ALCIBIADES' END

Alcibiades wasn't in Athens when it met its final defeat by the Spartans in 404 BC. By then he was in Asia Minor, where he was murdered: no one is sure who killed him – it might have been his old friends the Spartans, or his new ones, the Persians. Swapping sides had finally caught up with him.

DARIUS THE GREAT

Darius the Great grabbed the Persian throne for himself, then began a conquering spree that made the Persian Empire the biggest it would ever be.

HARD NUT RATING: 8.5

DARIUS TAKES CHARGE

Darius was born in 550 BC, during the reign of another great Persian conqueror, King Cyrus II. Darius was a distant relative of the king, and his father ruled one of the Persian provinces, but Darius had no claim to the throne. When King Cyrus died his son became king, but he was overthrown in 522 BC and someone else grabbed the throne. No one today is sure who it was, but according to Darius he was an evil imposter. So Darius killed him and took the throne himself.

REBELLIONS

Darius spent several busy years stopping troublesome rebellions that sprang up as a result of the change of ruler. He also wrote laws, fixed taxes, sorted out currency, built roads and set up trade routes. But he still found time for conquering. His generals conquered Thrace, Macedonia, the Punjab and quite a bit of the Indus Valley. Libya was made a province of the mighty Persian Empire too.

HARDOMETER

CUNNING: 9
COURAGE: 8
SURVIVAL SKILLS: 8
RUTHLESSNESS: 9

ANGRY GREEKS

In 507 BC, Darius made an alliance with Athens, but it wasn't long before the Greeks started getting fed up with the Persians – it was pretty obvious that if the Persians had their way, Greece would become part of the Persian Empire too. In 499 BC, the Persian Wars – between Persia and allied Greek city-states – began, and carried on for fifty years.

PERSIA INVADES

Darius and his army invaded Greece, and it was nearly ten years until the Greeks finally got rid of them at the Battle of Marathon (see page 46). Darius began making plans for a second invasion, and this time he planned to sack his generals and take command of the army himself. But in 486 BC he was stopped – not by the Greeks, but by illness, which killed him.

INVASION NUMBER TWO TO DO

ANCIENT GREEK MYTHOLOGY

The ancient Greeks worshipped twelve main gods and goddesses. They included the king of the gods, Zeus, Poseidon, god of the sea, Aphrodite, goddess of love, and Athene, goddess of wisdom. In Greek mythology the gods and goddesses often did bad things, and they were always interfering in human affairs. The ancient Greeks' stories about gods, goddesses, human heroes, monsters and strange beasts, are some of the best ever told. Here are just a few:

THE TWELVE LABOURS OF HERACLES

Heroic Heracles was punished by the gods by having to complete twelve tricky tasks, including killing a nine-headed watersnake, stealing man-eating horses, fetching Cerberus the three-headed guard dog from the Underworld, and capturing monstrous bulls, boar and deer.

THESEUS AND THE MINOTAUR

Theseus, Prince of Athens, killed the hideous bull-headed monster, the Minotaur, that lurked inside a special labyrinth on the island of Crete. The Athenians had to sacrifice seven boys and girls to the Minotaur every nine years, so the children of Athens were especially pleased to hear it had been killed.

PERSEUS AND MEDUSA

Perseus had to kill the Gorgon, Medusa, a monstrous woman with snakes for hair who was so ugly that anyone who looked at her would instantly turn to stone. Perseus was helped by the gods Hermes and Athene, and looked at her reflection in a magic shield when he cut her head off, so that he wasn't turned to stone.

HELEN OF TROY

Paris, Prince of Troy, had to judge which of three goddesses was the most beautiful. He chose Aphrodite, the goddess of love, who promised him the world's most beautiful woman in return. Unfortunately, the world's most beautiful woman, Helen, was already married. When she ran off with Paris, it started the Trojan War between Greece and Troy, which lasted ten years. It finally ended when the Greeks surprised the Trojans by leaping out of an enormous wooden horse that the Trojans thought was a gift.

DRACO

Draco was an Athenian who laid down the law – the criminals of Athens needed to watch out.

HARD NUT RATING: 7.3

NOT A SOFTIE

Draco was born some time in the 600s BC. We don't know anything about his life, but we can only guess that his hobbies didn't include flower arranging, embroidery, and cuddling kittens. What he is known for are the laws that he wrote down for the constitution of Athens – and they are pretty fierce.

ROUGH JUSTICE

Before Draco, laws were in the hands of an elite group who passed judgement if a crime was committed. It was probably a very unfair system – who was to say that the judges weren't just making things up as they went along, or delivering harsh punishments to people just because they didn't like the look of them? Draco's laws, written around 621 BC, made things clearer – but they were harsh. They gave death as the punishment for just about everything. If someone stole a cabbage, you might expect them to get a good telling-off and perhaps a bit of community service. But under Draco's laws, they'd be executed.

HARDOMETER

CUNNING: 6
COURAGE: 6
SURVIVAL SKILLS: 8
RUTHLESSNESS: 9

WORSE THAN DEATH

Apart from the moral question of whether it's right to kill people for minor offences (or even major ones), if death is the punishment for stealing as well as for murdering someone, a thief might be tempted to murder someone to avoid getting caught. However, these problems didn't seem to bother Draco. When he was questioned about the harshness of his punishments, he replied that he thought death was the correct punishment for the minor crimes, and he couldn't think of a more severe punishment for the serious ones. Another harsh punishment was for people who owed money – as long as they belonged to a lower social class, they could be sold into slavery.

DRACONIAN

It wasn't all bad. Well, it was mostly. But Draco did also change things so that more people had a say in politics. Later, the politician Solon got rid of all Draco's laws, except the one for murder. Today the word 'draconian' describes rules that are unnecessarily harsh.

LIST
OF
LAWS

PERICLES

Pericles was a tough nut general and politician who's remembered for making Athens the greatest city-state in Greece.

HARD NUT RATING: 7.3

PERSIAN INVADERS

As a child Pericles lived through troubled times: he was three when the Persians invaded Greece and were defeated at the Battle of Marathon (see page 46). Ten years later, Pericles might have been one of the children evacuated from Athens when it was pillaged by the Persians.

GETTING THE BUILDERS IN

The war with Persia was still going on when Pericles was first elected Athens' general in 458 BC. When it finally ended in 449 BC, Pericles decided to spend time making Athens the most beautiful, and also the most powerful, of all the Greek city-states. In 447 BC work began on the Parthenon, the marble temple on top of the Acropolis that's still there today, along with lots of other impressive and expensive buildings. To pay for it, Pericles used the money given to Athens by its allies, the city-states in the Delian League.

HARDOMETER

CUNNING: 8
COURAGE: 7
SURVIVAL SKILLS: 6
RUTHLESSNESS: 8

SPARTA GETS CROSS

Lots of people from the rest of the Delian League resented having to pay for all these lovely buildings in Athens. Most resentful of all were ancient Greek tough nuts the Spartans, and it was never a good idea to get on the wrong side of them. Pericles encouraged Athens to go to war with Sparta, and in 431 BC they did.

SEA BATTLES

Pericles decided that the best way to win the war was to retreat inside the city walls and avoid land battles with Sparta. Instead he would batter them at sea with the superior Athenian navy. His plan seemed to be working, and Pericles was especially good at giving rousing speeches to make the Athenians confident of winning and proud of their polis. But then something happened that Pericles hadn't predicted . . .

PLAGUE AND PESTILENCE

Athens was struck by plague. The disease spread quickly and dead bodies piled up in the streets as tens of thousands of people died. In 429 BC, Pericles himself became one of the plague's victims. The war with Sparta continued for another 25 years, and in the end Athens lost.

WELL I DIDN'T SEE THIS ONE COMING.

PYRRHUS

Pyrrhus was a king who couldn't resist a fight, but nearly lost everything when he tried to put a stop to the conquering Romans.

HARD NUT
RATING: 7.5

KING OF EPIRUS

Pyrrhus' father was the King of Epirus in northwestern Greece, but he was overthrown and killed when Pyrrhus was two. Luckily, Pyrrhus was whisked away by a friendly relative, who kindly invaded Epirus when Pyrrhus had grown up and restored him to his throne.

PTOLEMY'S HOSTAGE

You couldn't trust anyone in those days. While Pyrrhus was away at a wedding, someone else nicked his throne and so Pyrrhus went to stay with his sister and her husband, Demetrius (who happened to be the King of Asia). After a few battles and a marriage to the daughter of Ptolemy I, an Egyptian ruler, Pyrrhus sailed back to Epirus with a large army and navy supplied by Ptolemy. He quickly grabbed back his throne and, after killing his second cousin, became the sole King of Epirus once again.

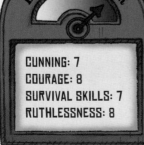

HARDOMETER

CUNNING: 7
COURAGE: 8
SURVIVAL SKILLS: 7
RUTHLESSNESS: 8

MARAUDING ROMANS

By this time the city of Rome had started to expand its territory by conquering the rest of Italy. A Greek city in southern Italy, Tarentum, called for Pyrrhus's help against the attacking Romans. Pyrrhus crossed the sea to Italy in 280 BC with around 20,000 men and a surprise.

PYRRHUS'S GIANT SURPRISE

Pyrrhus' surprise was war elephants. The Romans had never seen them before and were terrified. The giant animals helped Pyrrhus win. But the battle was a bloody one and Pyrrhus lost countless men – he's reported to have said that if he had another victory like that one it would be the end of him. Today, people still use the expression 'Pyrrhic victory' to mean a victory won at a terrible cost.

MORE FIGHTING

Never one to say no to a punch-up, Pyrrhus had further battles with the Romans, who finally defeated him in 275 BC, as well as the Carthaginians, the Macedonians, and the Spartans. He was killed in a riot in Argos in 272 BC.

CLEON

Cleon was a hard nut Athenian who absolutely hated the Spartans, and led Athens into bloody battles.

HARD NUT
RATING: 8

SPARTA AND PERICLES

The Peloponnesian War between Athens and Sparta was in full swing by the time Cleon became an Athenian politician. As well as hating the Spartans, Cleon really didn't like Pericles (see page 40) either – it was Pericles' policy of avoiding land battles with Sparta that annoyed him most. He accused Pericles of dodgy dealings with public money and managed to get him removed from his position of power, but only for a while. Finally, Pericles did Cleon a favour by dying of the plague in 429 BC.

MYTILENE

With Pericles out of the way, Cleon became the top politician in Athens and he soon had an uprising to deal with. In 428 BC the city-state of Mytilene on the island of Lesbos had the cheek to rebel. The Athenians quickly put a stop to it, but Cleon wanted to teach them a lesson they wouldn't forget. Proving his ruthless hard-nut credentials, he suggested that the entire male population of Mytilene should be executed. Luckily, other Athenians had a say in what happened. Cleon almost got his way, but in the end only about a thousand Mytilene men were killed.

HARDOMETER

CUNNING: 7
COURAGE: 9
SURVIVAL SKILLS: 6
RUTHLESSNESS: 10

CAPTURING SPARTANS

Cleon's finest hour came in 425 BC when he managed to capture Spartan troops who'd become stranded on the island of Sphacteria after the Battle of Pylos. He and the general Demosthenes brought the Spartans back to Athens, and Cleon threatened to kill them all if Sparta tried one of its invasions (Sparta had a nasty habit of invading every year – then going away again to help with the harvest and sort out the slave population). His threat worked. The Athenians became much more confident of winning the war.

THE END OF THE WAR

But Cleon's triumph didn't last long. He was killed in 422 BC trying to recapture Amphipolis, a city once controlled by Athens that the Spartans had captured. Those pesky Spartans got him in the end. After he died, the general Nicias negotiated a peace deal with the Spartans, which would have really annoyed Cleon, and the fighting stopped – at least, for seven years.

WANTED

PHEIDIPPIDES

One of the hardest ancient Greeks of them all isn't famous for conquering or fighting, but for running.

HARD NUT RATING: 6.5

SPARTAN HELP

The Persians arrived in Greece in 490 BC intent on making as much of it as possible a part of the Persian Empire. Their army assembled on the plains near the city of Marathon, about 40 kilometres from Athens. When the Athenian army arrived to meet them, they could see they were outnumbered. So they sent a messenger, Pheidippides, to Sparta to ask for help. After he'd run all the way there, the Spartans said they'd help, but not straight away. Heaving a big sigh, Pheidippides turned around and headed back with the news, a round trip of about 250 kilometres in two days.

THE BATTLE OF MARATHON

The Athenians decided to attack the Persians without Spartan help. The Athenian general Miltiades probably came up with the cunning tactics that encircled the Persians, defeated them and forced them to run like mad back to their ships on the coast. Lots of them drowned in the swamps on the way, but plenty of them succeeded in making it to the ships and, despite the Athenians' best efforts, most of the ships headed out to sea.

HARDOMETER

CUNNING: 6
COURAGE: 9
SURVIVAL SKILLS: 6
RUTHLESSNESS: 5

MARATHON TO ATHENS

The victorious Athenians knew that if the Persian ships reached Athens before they did, the Athenians might hand over the city to the marauding invaders, assuming that the Persians had won. The story goes that Pheidippides ran the 40 kilometres to Athens with the news of the Athenian victory as fast as he could – despite the fact he'd just run a 250-kilometre-warm-up, plus the major battle he'd just fought. But Pheidippides was made of stern stuff. He made it in record time, gave the Athenians the good news, then dropped dead of exhaustion. The Athenian army arrived later, and the thwarted Persians headed for home.

MODERN MARATHONS

Pheidippides' run from Marathon to Athens might not be true, but marathon races today are based on the distance between Marathon and Athens. Every year a 250 kilometre race called the Spartathlon recreates Pheidippides' longer run to ask for Spartan help.

20KM
TO
ATHENS

XERXES THE GREAT

Xerxes was a Persian emperor intent on grabbing Greece. Although he won battles and pillaged Athens, he never succeeded in making Greece part of his empire.

HARD NUT
RATING: 7.5

INHERITING AN EMPIRE

Xerxes was the son of hard nut Darius the Great (see page 34), and came to the throne when his father died in 486 BC. He started as he meant to go on – by making sure everyone knew he was ruthless, fierce and, most importantly, in charge. He began by battering Egypt and Babylon (which were both under Persian control).

WHIPPING UP A STORM

Next Xerxes turned his attention to one of his father's favourite projects: invading Greece. He amassed an army and navy and made boat bridges across the Hellespont, the narrow stretch of sea that links the Mediterranean with the Sea of Marmaris. A storm destroyed the bridges, and the story goes that Xerxes was so furious he looked for someone to blame. He decided the sea was responsible, so he whipped it with chains to teach it a lesson. It must have worked, because Xerxes' men remade the bridges and the Persian army crossed over into Greece.

HARDOMETER

CUNNING: 6
COURAGE: 7
SURVIVAL SKILLS: 7
RUTHLESSNESS: 10

PILLAGING PERSIANS

The first major battle with the allied Greeks was at the narrow mountain pass of Thermopylae. The Persians won, after a long and bloody battle, but suffered heavy losses at the hands of Spartan leader and self-sacrificing toughie, Leonidas (see page 14). But Xerxes did manage to invade and occupy Attica – the area surrounding Athens – and pillaged Athens itself in 480 BC, wrecking the Acropolis and setting fire to Athenian monuments.

PERSIANS GO HOME

Despite making himself extremely unpopular throughout Greece, Xerxes never became its emperor. The Persian fleet was defeated at the Battle of Salamis, which was the beginning of the end for Persian invasion plans. Xerxes lost interest in grabbing Greece after that, and eventually the Persians left Greece completely.

MURDER

Xerxes spent the rest of his life in the Persian cities of Susa and Persepolis. But rampaging conquerors rarely get to live out their days in peace, and in 465 BC Xerxes was murdered by treacherous members of his royal court.

PELOPIDAS

Pelopidas was a Theban warrior who created one of the fiercest fighting units in history, the Sacred Band of Thebes. They beat the toughest Greek warriors of the lot, the Spartans.

HARD NUT RATING: 9

THEBES AND SPARTA

Around twenty years after the end of the Peloponnesian war, Thebes was a wealthy city-state and an ally of Sparta. Pelopidas fought alongside the Spartans as a young man in 385 BC, against the Arcadians at the Battle of Mantinea. He was badly wounded but saved by his pal Epaminondas.

SPARTA TAKES OVER

Thebes and Sparta didn't stay friends for long and, with the help of a group of traitorous Thebans, Spartans captured the fortress of Thebes, the Cadmea, and took over the city-state. Pelopidas went into exile in Athens, where he spent his time persuading other Theban exiles to drive the Spartans out of Thebes. In 379 BC he led a brave band of rebels against the new Theban rulers, killed the lot and chucked out the Spartans.

HARDOMETER

CUNNING: 9
COURAGE: 10
SURVIVAL SKILLS: 8
RUTHLESSNESS: 9

THE SACRED BAND OF THEBES

Sparta planned its revenge, but Pelopidas was ready for them. He formed an elite fighting force of 300 young men known as the Sacred Band of Thebes. They were highly trained warriors, tough as old boots, and united in their aim to defend Thebes or die trying. Pelopidas and his men defeated Spartan troops when they met at the Battle of Tegyra, which only made the Spartans more determined. A 10,000-strong Spartan army marched on Thebes in 371 BC. The Theban army met them at Leuctra, commanded by Pelopidas' old pal Epaminondas. Pelopidas led the Sacred Band, and despite being outnumbered by the Spartans, the Thebans won.

TYRANT TROUBLE

Pelopidas' reputation as a hard nut meant that Thessaly asked for his help against the tyrant Alexander of Pherae, who was to become very troublesome for Pelopidas. His army defeated Alexander, and drove the Macedonians out of Thessaly for good measure.

PELOPIDAS' END

But in 364 BC Pelopidas was fighting Alexander once again. This time his troops won the battle, but Pelopidas was so keen to finish off Alexander himself that he rushed headlong into the tyrant's bodyguards and was killed.

HIPPOCRATES

Hippocrates was a doctor who made such an impact that 2,500 years later, new doctors still swear an oath named after him.

HARD NUT
RATING: 6.3

TRAVELLING DOCTOR

Hippocrates was born around 460 BC on the island of Kos. He travelled around Greece tending to sick people and training new doctors. His methods made him famous, and doctors who came after him continued to use his ideas for treating patients. He was one of the first doctors to realise that diseases had a natural cause – most people believed that they were caused by the gods or evil spirits. Before Hippocrates, sick people would probably be taken to a temple, or given some lucky charms, neither of which was likely to make them any better.

GETTING IT WRONG

Hippocrates did get one or two things wrong. He thought that diseases were caused by a bad diet, so he prescribed medicine to make patients sick and get rid of the disease-causing food. He also believed there were four 'humours' in the human body that had to be kept in balance, so treatment might mean draining a patient's blood to keep the humours balanced. Doctors were still doing that up until about 200 years ago!

HARDOMETER

CUNNING: 4
COURAGE: 9
SURVIVAL SKILLS: 8
RUTHLESSNESS: 4

GETTING IT RIGHT

Hippocrates did get a lot of things right, though. He was the first person to make systematic observations of diseases and keep careful records – methods that sound obvious but weren't at the time, and of course are still used today. He was the first to describe diseases including pneumonia, malaria, tetanus and tuberculosis. He also made a point of getting to know his patients, and treating them sympathetically, which helped some people to get better.

SNIFFING SICK

Hippocrates must have been made of stern stuff, because some of his methods were not for the faint-hearted: he tasted patients' wee and earwax, examined their sweat to see if it was sticky, and studied and smelled poo, snot and vomit. Despite that, he lived until he was 85, and became the most famous (and brave) doctor ever.

I SUSPECT THE COMMON COLD!

PISISTRATUS

Pisistratus slashed, bludgeoned, plotted and ambushed his way into becoming the tyrant of Athens.

HARD NUT RATING: 8.5

POLITICS

In the 500s BC there were bitter arguments about how Athens should be run. Two powerful rivals, Lycurgus and Megacles, opposed one another. Around 565 BC, when Athens was at war with Megara, Pisistratus became famous for capturing the enemy's harbour, and made the most of his popularity by setting up his own rival group.

TYRANT OF ATHENS

As a dramatic and bloody hard-nut publicity stunt, Pisistratus slashed his own body and drove into Athens' marketplace to show everyone how his enemies had wounded him. The trick worked: the people of Athens voted in favour of Pisistratus having a bodyguard armed with clubs. Cunning Pisistratus lost no time in using the club-wielding men to help him take over the Acropolis (Athens' citadel) by force. He was now the first tyrant of Athens – which meant a leader who was in charge because he'd fought his way to the top.

HARDOMETER

CUNNING: 9
COURAGE: 8
SURVIVAL SKILLS: 9
RUTHLESSNESS: 8

EXILED AND ANGRY

But it didn't last long. Pisistratus' two main rivals, Lycurgus and Megacles, managed to chuck him out after about a year. Pisistratus went to live in exile in northern Greece, where he spent his time growing rich from silver and gold mines, gaining support from like-minded rich people, putting his own personal army together, and plotting.

SURPRISE ATTACK

In 546 BC Pisistratus marched towards Athens with his army and launched an attack on the Athenian army just when they were least expecting it – in the heat of midday, when half of them were asleep. He quickly defeated the Athenian army and marched into Athens, as its tyrant once again.

POPULAR PISISTRATUS

Once in charge, Pisistratus did lots of impressive and useful building, encouraged poetry and music, and – unusual for an ancient Greek hard nut – he didn't wage any wars. True, he did take hostages from powerful families and keep them on the island of Naxos, and he kept a very scary bodyguard.

But generally Pisistratus was popular, and remained Athens' tyrant until he died in 527 BC.

Zzzzzzz

PERDICCAS

Perdiccas was a Macedonian general who ruled Alexander the Great's huge empire. He was ruthless and tough, but became too big-headed for his own good.

HARD NUT RATING: 7.3

GENERAL PERDICCAS

Perdiccas was one of Alexander the Great's (see page 12) most trusted generals. He earned a reputation as a brilliant warrior while Alexander's army was battering Thebes into submission in 335 BC, and was badly wounded there. He went on to command Alexander's cavalry campaigns in India.

ENORMOUS EMPIRE

Alexander died in 323 BC when he was only 32, leaving an empire that stretched from Egypt to India, and Perdiccas thought he should be the man to rule it. Alexander's brother was made king alongside Alexander's unborn baby, but because he wasn't well enough to rule and Alexander's baby was a bit young, Perdiccas got his way and became regent, ruling in their place.

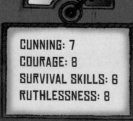

HARDOMETER

CUNNING: 7
COURAGE: 8
SURVIVAL SKILLS: 6
RUTHLESSNESS: 8

REVOLTING GENERALS

Lots of people didn't like the idea of Perdiccas running things, especially since he planned to marry Alexander's sister, meaning he would have better claim to rule the empire than anyone else. But first there was conquering to do. Cappadocia (in modern-day Turkey) was one of the few places Alexander hadn't conquered, so Perdiccas invaded straight away. He was expecting help from Antigonus, the governor of Phrygia, but it never came. Perdiccas summoned Antigonus to stand trial for disobedience but, sensibly, Antigonus ran away to Perdiccas' rivals, three men called Antipater, Craterus and Ptolemy, who had all been Alexander's generals as well. They agreed to revolt against Perdiccas.

MUTINY

Perdiccas left a friend to defend Asia against Antipater and Craterus while he marched on Ptolemy in Egypt. Ptolemy's army stopped him from crossing the River Nile, and some of Perdiccas' men were swept away in the river. Perdiccas' troops had had enough: he was a harsh leader, and now they were stuck uselessly on the banks of the Nile because of him. Finally, three of Perdiccas' officers assassinated him.

HARD NUTS OF ANCIENT GREECE TIMELINE

AROUND 800-500 BC

People had been living in Greece for thousands of years, and different civilizations came and went. In this period, Greece expanded into colonies around the Mediterranean, the first Olympic Games were held, and Athens became the biggest and richest city-state.

600S BC

Draco, who made some very harsh laws in Athens, was born some time in the 600s.

570 BC

Cleisthenes, the leader who introduced democracy to Athens, was born around this date.

550 BC

Persian ruler Darius the Great was born – and invaded Greece when he'd grown up.

527 BC

Pisistratus, the hard-nut tyrant of Athens, died.

524 BC

Themistocles was born around this date. He created a powerful Athenian navy that saw off the Persians.

519 BC

Xerxes the Great, Persian Emperor, was born around this date.

AROUND 500–336 BC

This period is known as the Classical Age, when Greek culture flourished.

499–449 BC

The Persian Wars between Persia and Greece – the allied Greek city-states eventually drove out the Persians.

495 BC

Athenian general Pericles was born around this date. He led Athens in the war with Sparta, and is remembered for making Athens great.

490 BC

Pheidippides died after running the first ever Marathon.

480 BC

Leonidas, the self-sacrificing Spartan warrior, died fighting the Persians.

470 BC

The philosopher Socrates was born around this date. He poisoned himself with hemlock at his own execution.

460 BC

Sick-sniffing doctor, Hippocrates, was born around this date.

450 BC

Alcibiades, the general who fought for both Athens and Sparta, was born around this date.

431–404 BC

The Peloponnesian Wars, fought between Athens and Sparta. In the end, Sparta won.

422 BC

Athenian general Cleon died in battle against the Spartans.

395 BC

Spartan leader Lysander died. He commanded the fleet that finally ended the Peloponnesian War.

371 BC

Thebes defeated Sparta to become the leading Greek city-state.

365 BC

Perdiccas was born around this date. He was Alexander the Great's general, who went on to command a huge chunk of the empire.

364 BC

Theban warrior Pelopidas died fighting the tyrant Alexander of Pherae.

356 BC

Unstoppable conqueror Alexander the Great was born.

338 BC

Philip II of Macedonia became ruler of Greece.

319 BC

Pyrrhus, King of Epirus, was born. He fought the conquering Romans, but at a cost.

290 BC

Archimedes, the inventor and mathematician, was born around this date.

146 BC

Greece became part of the Roman Empire.

415 AD

Brilliant mathematician and astronomer Hypatia was killed.

GLOSSARY

AGOGE A military boarding school where Spartan men trained to be warriors

ALLIANCE An agreement between different countries or nations to work together in order to achieve something

ARCHON 'Leader' or 'lord' – the top political job in ancient Athens

ASSASSINATED Murdered in a surprise attack (usually for political reasons)

BESIEGED Surrounded by enemy forces

BLOCKADED Closed off by enemy forces so that people cannot enter or leave

COLONIES Territories that are under the control of another state or country

CONSTITUTION A set of national laws according to which a country is governed

CORRUPTING Ruining someone's good character by encouraging them to do something wrong

DEMOCRACY A form of government where leaders are elected (chosen) by the people of the state or country

EXILE Being banned from your native country

FLEET A group of warships

HEMLOCK A highly poisonous plant

HUMOURS The four fluids of the human body (black bile, yellow bile, phlegm and blood). An imbalance of the humours was thought to cause ill health

IMPOSTER A person who pretends to be someone else

MASSACRED Brutally killed

MEGALOMANIAC A person who has an obsessive desire for great power or wealth

PENINSULA A piece of land sticking out from the mainland so that it is surrounded by water on three sides

PERSECUTED Ill treated due to political or religious beliefs

POLIS An Ancient Greek city-state

REGENT Someone who is temporarily acting as a head of state

THWARTED Stopped from doing something

TYRANT A harsh and cruel leader

INDEX